Waiting for Baby

Patricia A. Anderson

Waiting for Baby

This book is written to provide information and motivation to readers. Its purpose is not to render any type of psychological, legal, or professional advice of any kind. The content is the sole opinion and expression of the author, and not necessarily that of the publisher.

Copyright © 2021 by Patricia A. Anderson.

All rights reserved. No part of this book may be reproduced, transmitted, or distributed in any form by any means, including, but not limited to, recording, photocopying, or taking screenshots of parts of the book, without prior written permission from the author or the publisher. Brief quotations for noncommercial purposes, such as book reviews, permitted by Fair Use of the U.S. Copyright Law, are allowed without written permissions, as long as such quotations do not cause damage to the book's commercial value. For permissions, write to the publisher, whose address is stated below.

Printed in the United States of America.

ISBN 978-1-955363-60-0 (Paperback)
ISBN 978-1-955363-61-7 (Digital)

Lettra Press books may be ordered through booksellers or by contacting:

Lettra Press LLC
30 N Gould St. Suite 4753
Sheridan, WY 82801
1 307-200-3414 I info@lettrapress.com
www.lettrapress.com

"What's this?" Devind asked, as he picked up the ultra sound picture of the sixteen week old fetus that would be his cousin.

"It's a picture of your new cousin. Uncle David and Aunt Cheryl are going to have a baby." explained Grandma.

"It sure looks funny." said Devind as he turned the picture sideways and upside down, trying to see anything that resembled a baby.

"That's because the baby isn't born yet. It is still growing."

"Where are they growing it?" he asked curiously.

"The baby is in Aunt Cheryl's uterus." Grandma said, knowing this wasn't the last of Devind's questions.

"What's a uterus?" Devind continued.

"It's a special place inside Aunt Cheryl's belly where the baby will grow until it's time for him or her to be born." Grandma explained patiently.

Won't it be crowded in there?" Devind asked with a worried look on his face.

"No. Aunt Cheryl's belly will grow as the special place grows. That way the baby will have plenty of room to grow too."

"How will it get out when it's ready to be born?" was the next question Devind thought needed to be answered.

Through a birth canal. That's a special opening just for babies to be born." Grandma explained, wondering if Devind was understanding anything she was saying.

"Oh." he said. Then he thought a while before asking, "Is that where I was before I was born?"

"Yes. Only you were inside Mommy's uterus, not Aunt Cheryl's."

"Oh." Devind said again, as he tried to think of other questions he needed to have answered about his new cousin. "How can the baby breathe in there?" he finally asked.

"Through the umbilical cord. That's how belly buttons are made. It's like a straw that the baby can get air though, much the same way you can get milk through your straw. Once the baby is born, it can breathe air like we do so the doctor makes a belly button out of it."

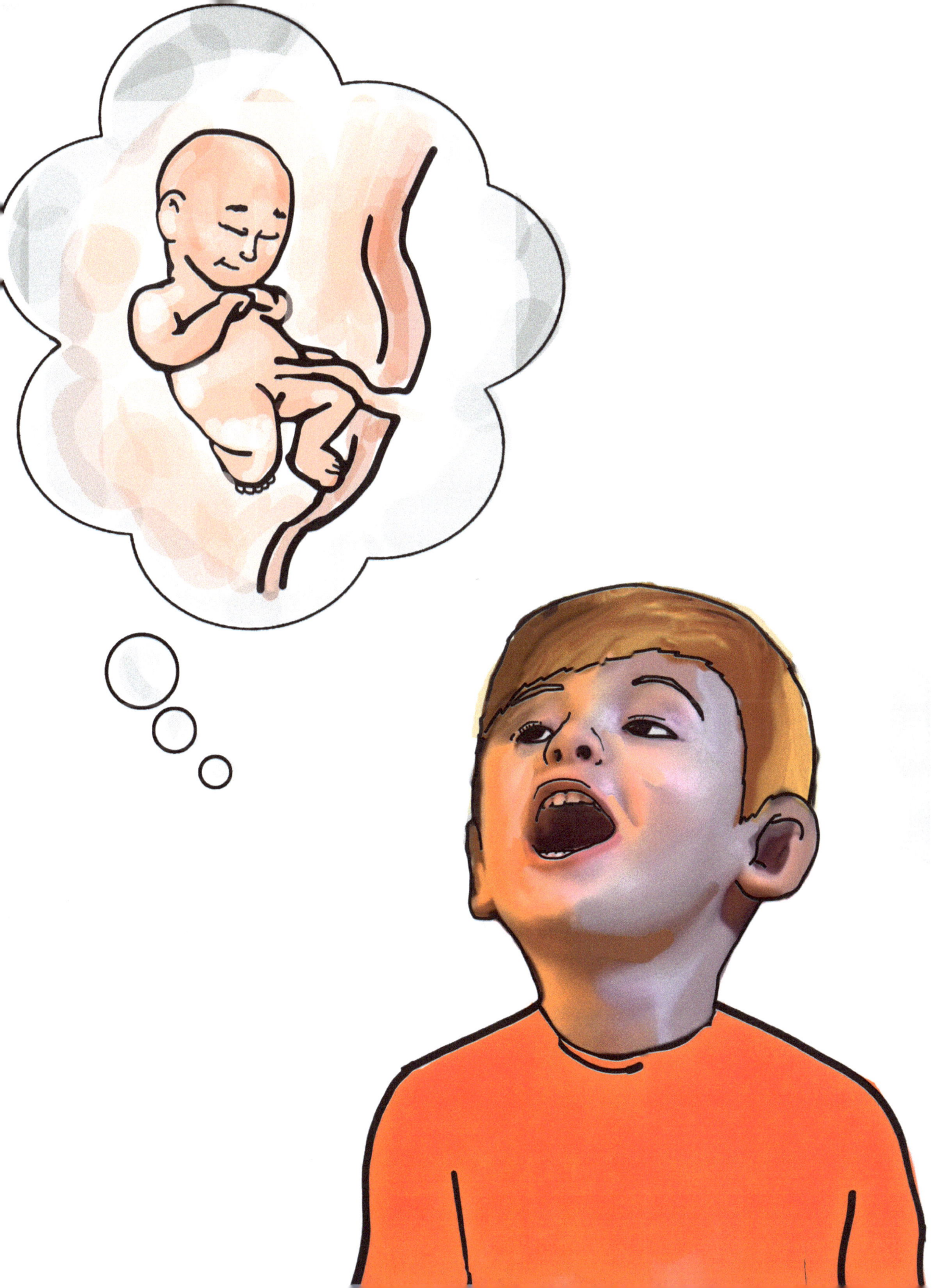

Devind looked at the picture again and studied it for a long time. Finally he seemed to see something that looked like a baby. "Look Grandma, that looks like feet!" he said excitedly.

"That's right." said Grandma, looking over his shoulder as he pointed to the feet of the fetus.

"It still looks funny. I hope they finish putting the baby together before my cousin gets here to visit us." he said shaking his head. "When is the baby gonna get here?"

Some time in April or early May." replied Grandma. "Think you can wait that long?"

"I guess I'm gonna hafta." he said with a not – so – very – happy look on his face.

Sure enough, Lucas was born in April. Grandma and Grandpa went to visit him and brought back pictures to share with the rest of the family. Devind was thrilled to see that his new little cousin was not only "finished" being made, but kind of cute too.

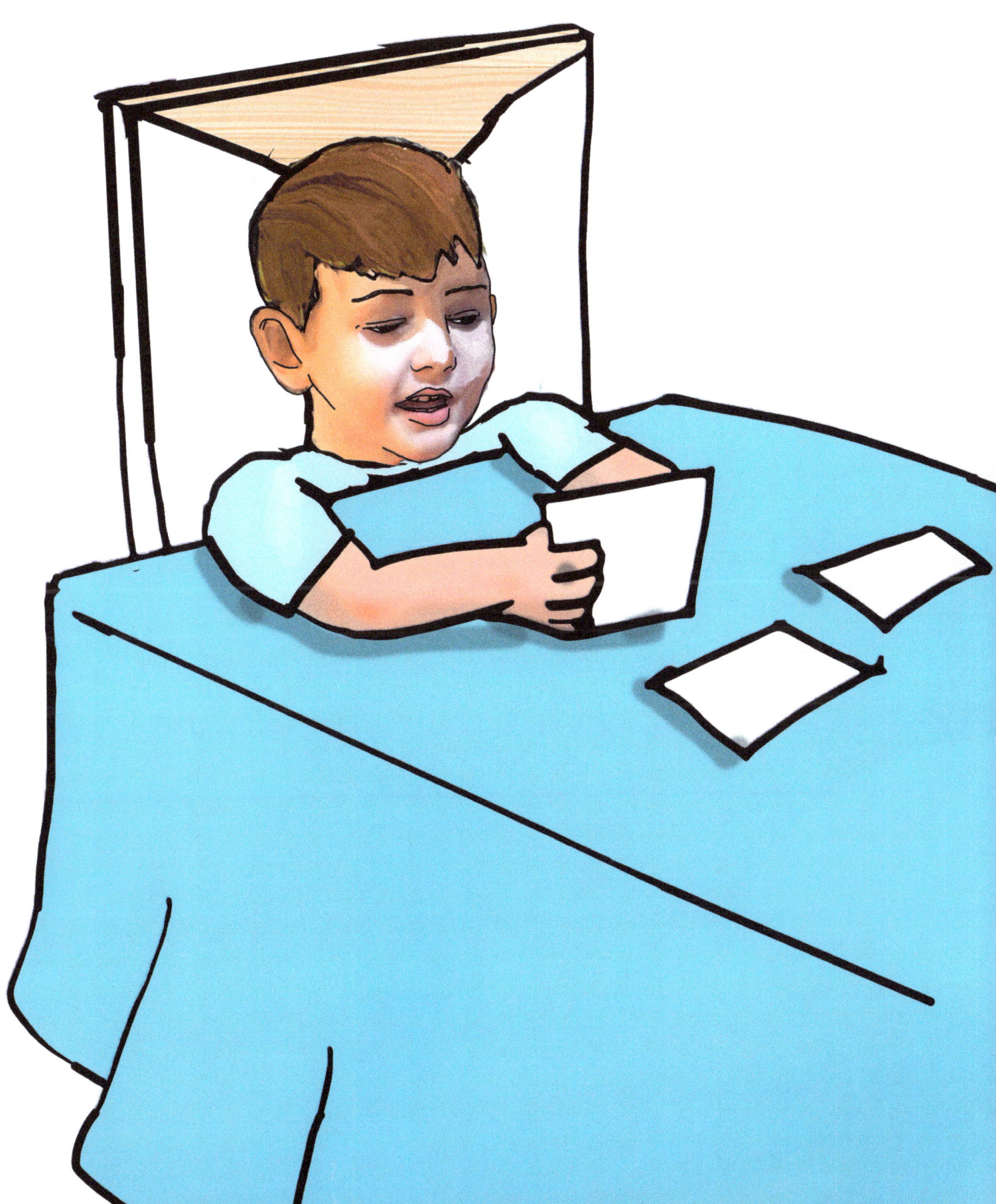

"Hey, can Lucas come and visit so we can play together?" asked Devind with the impatience of a four year old.

"Yes." Grandma replied. "But can you wait until he gets a little older? He can't quite play like you do right now?"

"Okay. I guess I'm gonna hafta." he said with his usual not – so – very – happy look on his face – again.

Meanwhile, he looked forward to the pictures of Baby Lucas that came via the emails from Uncle David and Aunt Cheryl, who lived a little to far away to visit.

Words You May Not Know
according to Devind

Fetus (fee- tus): What a baby is called before it's born.

Explained (x – plane – d): Told what something is.

Resembled (ree – zem – bell – d): A big word that means looks like.

Curiously (k – your – e – us – lee): Wanting to know.

Continued (con – tin – u – d): Kept going on and on.

Studied (sta – deed): Kept looking at it until it made sense.

Replied (ree – pli – d): Another word for answered.

Thrilled (ther – il – d): Another word for being happy.

Impatience (im – pay – shunce): A big word for not wanting to wait.

Via (vee – u [as in up]): The way something comes by, like mail, pictures or telephone.

Uterus (you – ter – us) A place in a Mommy's belly made just for babies.

Umbilical cord (um – bil – ick – al – kord) – A kind of tube that connects the Baby to the Mommy so it can get air, blood and food to grow.

Growing a Baby

You were kinda funny looking
    in the first picture I saw of you.
But everyone said you'd look
    much better, once you grew.
So I waited for a long, long time
    to see if they were right.
And then it happened, one day
    a new picture came to light.
And there you were, a baby boy
    you'd grown, and I could see
You were kinda cute looking
    and a part of our family.

www.ingramcontent.com/pod-product-compliance
Lightning Source LLC
Chambersburg PA
CBHW061108070526
44579CB00011B/177